www.booksbyboxer.com

Published by
Books By Boxer, Leeds, LS13 4BS UK
Books by Boxer (EU), Dublin D02 P593 IRELAND
© Books By Boxer 2021
All Rights Reserved
MADE IN MALTA
ISBN: 9781909732742

Rose Quartz

LOVE + COMPASSION + FRIENDSHIP

Friday night and all alone?
Dating profile getting no hits?

Your Rose Quartz has been touched by the office gossip and has absorbed their negative energy! Cleanse immediately!

Back in your safe hands, you've got a date with the office hottie and brunch with the girls. Rose Quartz amplifies and draws in love and kindness to deepen existing and blossoming new relationships with others and compassionate self-love.

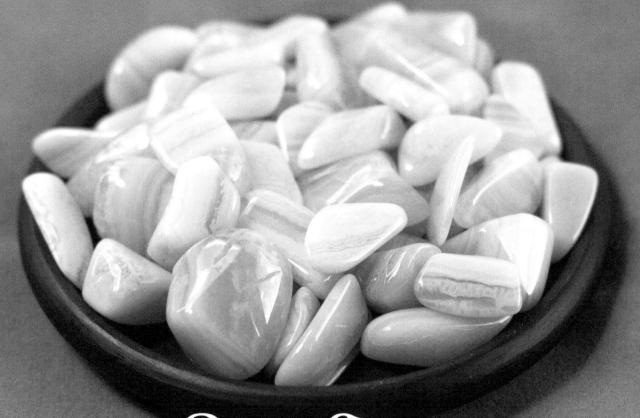

Blue Agate

COMMUNICATION + CONFIDENCE + CLARITY

Need to give someone a piece of your mind?

If you're sick of a certain busybody or need to tell your boss where to shove it, then Agate is the perfect solution!

With communication boosting abilities and the power to alleviate your tension and anger, you don't need to worry about making yourself heard.

Types of crystals:

✧Cut: Shaped to capture the light and beauty of the crystal.
The captured light enhances the crystal's energy.

✧Tumbled: Smooth to the touch, these round and shiny crystals are great to hold in your hand and carry around with you.

✧Wand: Shaped with a point at one end, you can use a wand-shaped crystal to direct energy into one direction.
Be warned that raw crystals hold much more power so use with caution.

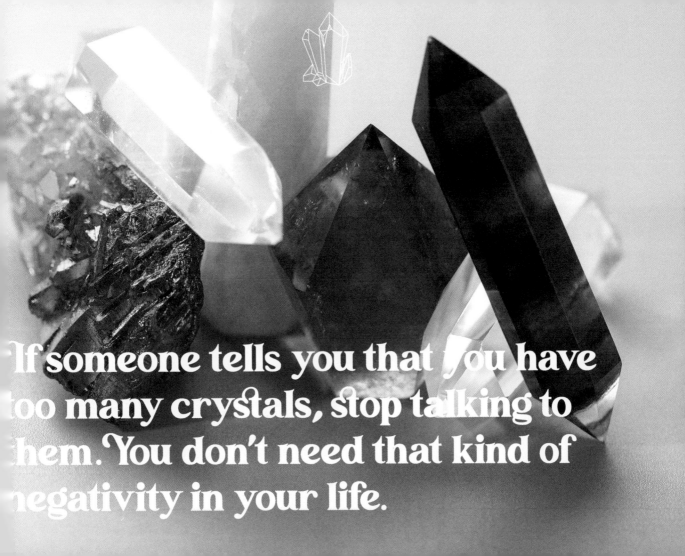

If someone tells you that you have too many crystals, stop talking to them. You don't need that kind of negativity in your life.

Hematite

GROUNDING + PROTECTION + BALANCING

Need a spring cleaning routine for bad vibes?

While you can't exactly hoover up negative energies, you can help obliterate bad vibes in both the home and your mind with a Hematite crystal.

Though dark in colour, Hematite is actually a purifying crystal, which helps to absorb bad energies, providing peace and balance to the home. This dark crystal also has abilities of grounding and protection, and can also boost confidence and self-esteem within its owner.

Malachite

TRANSFORMATION + POSITIVITY + PROTECTION

You're about to go into labour, whatever you do, don't forget to pick up your Malachite!

Are you in your third trimester of pregnancy? Calm those labour worries with Malachite! Known as the midwife's stone, Malachite is said to help stimulate contractions, ease labour pain and make way for a safe birth. Not just for pregnancy, this handy stone can ease period pains, absorb negative energies and pollutants, and encourage risk-taking and change!

Crystals can help you tap into your inner joy. Born from the earth, connected to energy, and radiant with high vibrations, these stones can be an awesome way to cleanse the chakras, digest your feelings, and find your ease and brightness in the world once more.

You can't buy happiness but you can buy crystals. And that's kind of the same thing, right?

Larimar

CALMING + TRANQUILITY + HEALING

Need to calm your inner bitch?

When somebody has rattled your cage and awoken your inner bitch, it can be hard to control your temper. As the embodiment of the tranquil sea and sky, Larimar's calming colours and energies help to calm fears, relieve stress and cool tempers.

It is said that Larimar is an enlightening, earth healing stone, which brings out the goddess energy in women.

Citrine

LUCK + CONFIDENCE + HAPPINESS

Can't find the pot at the end of the rainbow?

When you're feeling down on your luck, sometimes all you need is a confidence boost!

Gold in colour, it's no wonder Citrine attracts success and prosperity to the crystal's owner. This confidence enhancing crystal encourages happiness and riches to enter your life.

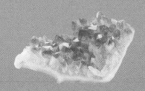

How to activate your crystal:

After cleansing your crystal, you will need to 'activate' it with your specific needs and intentions.

To do this, hold your crystal in your hand and set a clear intention for yourself.

My third eye can see right through your bullshit.

Clear Quartz

MASTER HEALER + BALANCING + GROWTH

Need an all round booster?

Falling asleep during boring meetings? Forgetting your keys?
If your body and mind need a boost, crystals can give your body
what it's lacking! Clear Quartz is the 'Jack of all trades' crystal.

With the power to aid concentration and memory, the Clear Quartz
can enhance your mind and body to work at the best of their ability!
Whatever energy this crystal absorbs, it amplifies the amount it releases.

Dragon's Blood Jasper

COURAGE + PROTECTION + SEXUAL AWARENESS

Going into battle on Monday morning? Need to wage war on your best friend's ex?

Historically given to warriors to grant them the courage of a ferocious dragon, Dragon's Blood Jasper is a handy little stone that will aid you in your journey of self discovery and courage, allowing you to set and achieve your goals in life.

Perfect for days when you've not had enough coffee but you need to stand your ground in the morning briefing against Karen from finance.

The Cullinan diamond was known as the largest gem diamond.

It weighed 3,106 carats, or nearly a pound and a half, when it was discovered in South Africa in 1905.

The Cullinan produced nine major stones as well as ninety-six brilliants.

Lapis Lazuli

WISDOM + HONESTY + STIMULATION

Preparing for an important exam?

Perhaps you have an assignment to finish, or maybe you need to practice for tonight's pub quiz. If you need to boost your knowledge, then the Lapis Lazuli is the stone for you.

Known as the wisdom stone, Lapis Lazuli won't help one bit when getting your wisdom teeth out, but it is great at enhancing self-awareness, deep peace and inner truth.

Rhodochrosite

ENERGISING + PASSION + LIFTING

Need to add some extra oomph to your life?

Is life feeling a little uneventful at the moment? Perhaps you're feeling a bit deprived of fun? Open your heart and mind to encourage positive attitudes and relationships to enter into your life with Rhodochrosite!

With the ability to simulate love and passion, all while leaving you feeling more energised, Rhodochrosite works like a treat to make everyday seem brighter.

What your crystal colours represent:

✧Black: Protection.   ✧Pink: Love.
✧Brown: Cleansing.   ✧Red: Energy.
✧White: Purity.   ✧Yellow: Wealth and plenty.
✧Green: Calming.

Dark colours focus on safeguarding their user.

I have more crystals than friends.

Black Obsidian

PROTECTION + TRANSFORMATION + BALANCING

Need to burn some bridges?

Sometimes you need to cleanse your life of toxicity. Maybe it's
a 'friend' who seems to drain your energy when they're around,
or an arsehole ex who keeps worming their way into your DMs.

Sever the ties with energy leeches and harmful relations with
Black Obsidian. This dark stone is great for protection against
negative people, making sure your energy isn't compromised
when they're around.

Green Jade

ABUNDANCE + HAPPINESS + PROTECTION

Fancy yourself a bit of a dreamer?

Some dreams can be an insight into your mind
(No, not the one about you marrying your fave celeb), and can
be useful in determining what you want from life.

Known as the dream stone, Green Jade helps to soothe the mind,
release negative thoughts and bring more insightful dreams
towards you. Not only that, but Green Jade is also great at
attracting harmony, good luck and friendship to its user.

How to cleanse your crystals - moon

Bathe crystals in cold water and lay them out on your windowsill overnight to soak up the rays of moonlight from a full moon.

Be aware that direct sunlight can cause some types crystals to fade, so be careful not to leave crystals out in strong rays of sunlight.

It's not hoarding,
I am simply raising my vibration.

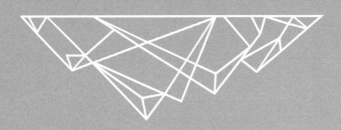

How to cleanse your crystals - smudge

Hold the crystal in your hand and set alight a bundle of sage or palo santo wood until it smoulders.

Then wave the smoke back and forth over the crystals, extinguishing any embers. This is typically best done outdoors to allow the smoke and negative energy to disperse.

Can I call you back?
I'm saging my crystal.

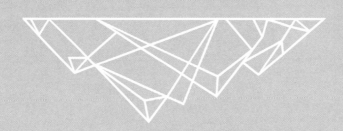

How to cleanse your crystals - rice

Cleansing your crystals will recharge their
power and reassert their intentions.

To rid your crystals of bad energy and
negativity (especially protective stones), bury your
stone in a bowl of dry, brown rice for up to 24 hours.

Throw away the rice immediately after the crystal's cleansing
as it will have absorbed the energy you're trying to eradicate.

Sorry, I can't.
It's a full moon
and I need to
charge my crystals!

How to cleanse your crystals - water

Collect rain water during the full moon to wash and supercharge your crystals for additional power, as it's important to keep your crystals connected to earth.

Be careful though, there are some crystals that can't be washed so always check before cleansing with water.

Did you ever stop to think, that maybe crystals are addicted to me?

Tigers Eye

HEALING + CONFIDENCE + BALANCING

Hate flying? Scared of spiders?

The Tiger's Eye stone is your go-to remedy for phobias and tensions (unless you have a fear of stones and crystals, that is).

With the ability to abolish fear and anxiety and create a calm and confident balance in your mind, Tiger's Eye is especially good for travellers who want to stay centered and calm on their journey!

Apatite

MOTIVATION + FOCUS + MANIFESTATION

Need to put on your walking shoes?

Whether you're wanting to participate in a 5k run, get to the gym more often or have a goal set in your mind, Apatite will have you achieving your personal best in no time!

When you need the motivation to get up and go, the Apatite stone will enhance your focus and motivation and help to manifest your goals.

Quartz crystals have a piezoelectric property that is widely used in electronics. Radios, microphones, robotics, timers, clocks, buzzers, watches, and many more electronic components and devices use Quartz crystals.

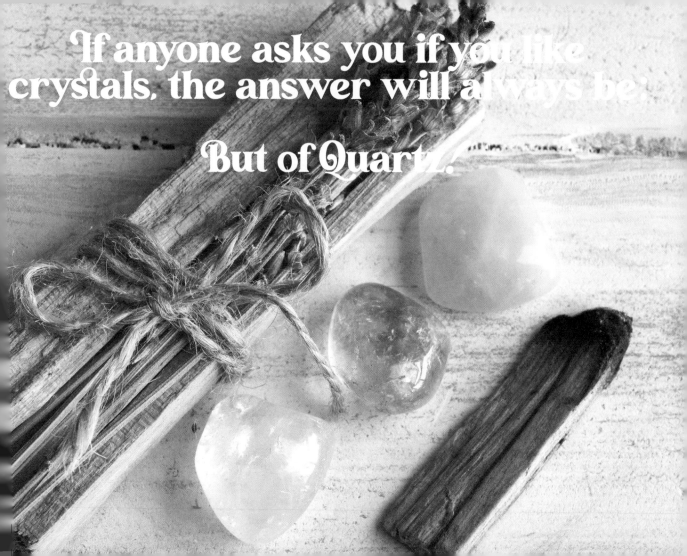

If anyone asks you if you like crystals, the answer will always be:

But of Quartz!

Bismuth

COMFORT + CALMING + SUPPORT

Saturday night plans fallen through?

Planned to go out with your besties? Have plans changed and now you're feeling a little lonely? Bismuth is the perfect relief for feelings of loneliness and isolation.

With an ability to help its user adapt easier to change with a calmer perspective, this colourful rock helps to comfort and support its owner. With an added benefit, Bismuth can also introduce order to the overwhelming chaos in your life, allowing for you to organise ideas and projects.

Carnelian

CREATIVITY + MOTIVATION + PASSION

In need of some passionate motivation?

Waiting for the motivation to get up and go? Perhaps that paint can is still sat unopened in your shed? Carnelian is your go-to stone when you want to get moving.

Perfect for inspiring motivation, creativity and passion in your life, Carnelian is useful when you want to take on a new project. Use this in the bedroom at your own risk though; Carnelian stimulates sexual energy and passion, and will make those sparks fly!

Ancient Egyptians considered green coloured gemstones such as Emeralds and Peridot to be very valuable and to have brought luck to the person wearing them.

Peridot and Emeralds were the favourites amongst the people of the bygone era. It is believed that Egyptian Queen Cleopatra favoured Peridot.

Emerald Scarab

Ametrine

OPTIMISM + WILLPOWER + GUIDANCE

Finding it hard to say no to another cream bun?

Has one of your colleagues brought doughnuts into the office again?

Get your hand out of the biscuit tin and your fingers round an Ametrine crystal! With powers to enhance your optimism and willpower, this beautiful crystal will give you guidance to keep on the right track.

White Howlite

PATIENCE + PEACE + FOCUS

Not getting enough beauty sleep?

Bedtime is a gamble. You either sleep like a baby or you toss and turn for hours, remembering every embarrassing moment in your life. When you find yourself struggling to sleep due to overthinking, simply pop a White Howlite stone under your pillow.

With soothing properties, this little stone calms overthinking minds and helps relieve stress and anxiety so you can get some well-deserved beauty sleep.

Zircon is the oldest crystal that has been found in the world. A tiny 4.4-billion-year-old zircon crystal has been confirmed as the oldest fragment of Earth's crust. The crystal was found in sandstone in the Jack Hills region of Western Australia. Scientists dated the crystal by studying its uranium and lead atoms.

Red Jasper

COURAGE + PROTECTION + SEXUAL AWARENESS

Taking things to the next level?

Want to take things further with your partner? Maybe you're nervous to reciprocate their advances or just want to add a little extra spice in the bedroom? Red Jasper can bring sexual awareness and pleasure to its user!

With the power to stimulate courage, aid in sexual pleasure and rid its owner of sexual related guilt, this deep red stone is great for passion and protection. Legends surrounding Red Jasper say that the stone drives away evil spirits and protects against spiders and snakes too!

Helitrope - Bloodstone

POWERFUL + HEALING + RESILIENCE

Procrastination becoming an issue?

When you have difficult tasks and looming deadlines, it's easy to fall into a pattern of starting a task and not seeing it through to the end. Helitrope (known as Bloodstone due to its red flecks), is the perfect motivator.

Enhancing your resilience and strength, you can bash through those exhausting tasks so you have more time to do your own thing!

Some believe that the name 'Garnet' was derived from a word meaning blood, but the blood-red coloured gemstone actually got its name from the pomegranate fruit because the fruit's blood-red seed is similar to a Garnet stone colour.

Natural Garnet

Aquamarine

SERENITY + RELAXATION + COURAGE

Desperate for five minutes peace and quiet?

When you're being driven to insanity by your kids or your workload is making you rage, take yourself off to a quiet room with an Aquamarine crystal to restore your serenity.

A protection stone for mothers and expectant mothers, Aquamarine boosts courage and helps release anger, stress and anxiety.

Amethyst

PEACE + STABILITY + CALM

Messed up an important presentation?
Forgot to send that important email?

Your Amethyst is still sitting on your windowsill cleansing
and isn't sitting on your desk bringing you clarity of mind.

Amethyst is a powerful protection stone, protecting the
wearer from harm and negative thoughts. It can soothe
anxiety, help with sleep and ensures good dreams.

Amber is considered to be the softest and lightest gemstone and is the result of resin and sap from fossilised prehistoric trees.

Baltic Amber is regarded as the strongest type of Amber and is used for creating Amber jewellery.

Baltic Amber

Tourmaline

PROTECTION + GROUNDING + MANIFESTING

Manifestations just not coming to fruition?

Gone through a bad break up? Or have a toxic ex whose words you can't seem to clear from your mind? You need Tourmaline.

Grounds from negative and unbalanced emotions to provide clarity and protection to the mind, Tourmaline protects against negative thoughts and people!

Amazonite

BALANCING + CALMING + TRUTH

Need to dampen your mood swings?

Do you find yourself being a little hot headed? Perhaps the person in front is walking a little too slow, or your partner left the toilet seat up yet again?

The Amazonite crystal helps to calm your temper, assist you in communicating effectively and will allow you to see situations from a different perpective.

Ammonites can be fossilised in such a way that they become a type of gemstone called Ammolite. It is one of only three biogenic gemstones, the others being Amber and Pearls.

Ammolite is growing in popularity, as it is used in Native American art, in Feng Shui, and as imitation Opals.

Ammolite

Orange Calcite

CONCENTRATION + INTELLIGENCE + JOY

Learning a new hobby?

Whether you're wanting to try your hand at playing the guitar, learn a new subject or try a new recipe, Orange Calcite can help improve your concentration, creativity and ability to learn.

With the ability to boost intelligence and reduce distractions, you'll be among the legends in no time! If you're wanting to get frisky with your partner, this crystal can help to spice things up, with its pleasure and sexual energy enhancing powers!

Jet - Black Amber

PROSPERITY + PROTECTION + RELEASE

Need to make your feelings known?

Still raging about the office lunch thief? Need to release your pent up emotions so you can forgive and move on? Jet helps draw out negative energy so you can focus on gaining control of your life and find a balance in your emotions.

This stone is effective in decreasing depression in its owner and makes a great protection stone. A physical, emotional and spiritual guidance enhancer, Jet can help you accomplish your goals so you can prosper!

Crystal gazing was a popular pastime in the Victorian era, and was claimed to work best when the sun had set in its most northern decline. Before a vision would appear it was said that the ball would mist up.

Romani fortune tellers often used a crystal ball to predict the future and fortunes of their clients.

If I had a crystal ball I'd sit down very carefully.

Celestite

CONNECTION + PURIFICATION + CALMING

Need some help from the other side?

If you've got connectivity issues when getting in touch with your spiritual side, Celestite might just be your solution!

Being in the presence of Celestite can enhance your psychic gifts and welcomes angels into your space. By radiating gentle calming and purifying energy, this crystal can also promote a good night's sleep.

Morganite

HEAL HEARTBREAK + EMPATHY + COMPASSION

In search of a spark of romance?

When you're single, sexy, and ready to take on the dating scene (either to have a little fun or hunt down your soulmate), make sure to take Morganite with you on your adventure!

A crystal with many powers, Morganite can boost courage, healing and compassion to face feelings of heartbreak and loss, helping you move on to better things. Associated with romance, this crystal will help you realise new potential in love, and maybe get you on a second date!

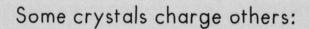

Some crystals charge others:

Crystal Quartz and Selenite are powerful stones that can be used to amplify the energy of any other stones they come in contact with.

Use a charging stand or another crystal and let them touch overnight. See if you notice a new brightness after charging them this way.

May the Quartz be with you.

Alexandrite

JOY + NOBILITY + HARMONISING

Need to find joy in everyday life?

Whether it's a trip to the supermarket, walking the dog or having a coffee with a friend, it's important to find joy in every day. The crystal Alexandrite helps to boost self-esteem and allows its user to find joy and harmony in every moment.

Well known as a symbol of royal power, this noble crystal reinforces and realigns the mind and spirit!

Amber

POSITIVITY + ROMANTIC LOVE + SENSUALITY

Got a blind date coming up?

When you're on the hunt for love, Amber will be your wingman! With a warming glow that radiates sensuality and luck, you can light the fire in your romance.

This passionate crystal helps to stimulate and manifest your deepest desires and works as a good luck charm in love and marriage!

Is there a specific purpose you would like to achieve with your crystal - physical or mental? Reflect on each crystals power and choose wisely.

If in doubt, choose from your gut, as you may feel a certain pull to a specific crystal - if it's right for you when in your hand you should feel a pull from in front of you.

However, if you fall back, then this is not your intended crystal so put it down and step away!

I have a crystal for that!

In need of a good night's sleep?

The following crystals can help purify your aura as well as soothe and relax the mind, encouraging a good night's sleep:

✧Fluorite.
✧Green Calcite.
✧Howlite.
✧Moonstone.
✧Amethyst.
✧Celestite.

Life is always rocky
when you're a gem.

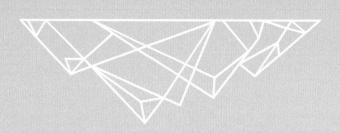

Want to land that promotion?

The following crystals can help give you clarity and boost your productivity levels to new heights!

✧Citrine.
✧Sodalite.
✧Pyrite.
✧Green Jade.
✧Carnelian.
✧Amazonite.

My magic crystal ball tells me you're full of shit.

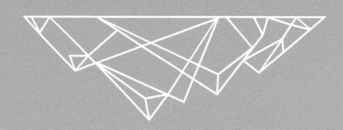

Lucking out on love?

The following crystals can help you open up your heart
to new possibilities as well as soothe and heal past heartache.

✧Rose Quartz.
✧Amethyst.
✧Aventurine.
✧Rhodochrosite.
✧Carnelian.
✧Lapis Lazuli.

Of course size matters,
no one wants a small
crystal collection.

Labradorite

PROTECTION + MYSTICAL + TRANSFORMATION

Is your mind going into overdrive?

Are you spending your days thinking about the ifs, buts and whys?
Help to calm your overactive mind with Labradorite!

With the power to deflect unwanted energy from entering your aura,
this glimmering stone helps to overcome your fears and anxiety and
calms your thoughts. With the added ability to aid your intuition and
mystical qualities, this stone is great for divination!

White Opal

MYSTICAL + HARMONISING + LOVE

Want to protect your heart from undeserving fuckboys and womanisers?

The dating scene is difficult. Avoiding lunatics and players like the plague is hard, but not entirely impossible. Protect yourself from danger and draw love and faithfulness towards you with a White Opal stone.

Perfect for wearing as a necklace, this beautiful stone guards from evil and brings protection from playful angels!

Rose Quartz is extremely popular in Feng Shui, and you will find a range of objects containing Rose Quartz that are used as love cures.

Mandarin ducks, wealth pots, hearts, pots and gourds tied with red string are particularly effective in Feng Shui if they are made from Rose Quartz.

The main reason for the stone's strength is the manganese and titanium it contains. This mineral content is particularly helpful in calming and healing the mind.

I just ate like six Rose Quartz stones and nobody's in love with me yet.

What gives?

Peridot

STRENGTH + BALANCE + HARMONISING

Bad dreams affecting your beauty sleep?

There's nothing worse than being woken up from sleep by nightmares of being chased, going bald or your Wi-Fi disconnecting! An anxiety reducing crystal, Peridot brings a calming effect to its owner and helps to bring strength and balance to your life.

With abilities to protect its user from negative emotions like sadness and anger, Peridot can be used to gain more restful sleep.

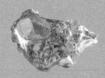

Snowflake Obsidian

BALANCE + PURIFY + GROUNDING

Need help through difficult times?

Does your life feel upside down? Maybe you've just had a breakup or found out some shocking news about your favourite celebrity couple. Snowflake Obsidian can help ground and purify energy, so you can have a good emotional balance once again.

Considered a stone for manifestation, Snowflake Obsidian helps to balance your mind, body and spirit and can keep negative energy from affecting you, so you can focus more on the good things and get your life back on track!

Tanzanite is a rare blue/violet stone that can only be found at Mt Kilimanjaro in Tanzania. The stone stands out because of its "trichroism", meaning that the stone changes colour from blue to violet when turned in the light.

In its rough state, Tanzanite is a purple/brown colour and is therefore heat treated to bring out the blue/violet tones.

Uncut Tanzanite

Moldavite

GROWTH + TRANSFORMATION + AWAKENING

Wondering what your destined path in life is?

Are you unsure if the route you're taking in life is meant for you? While effective in boosting your transformation and growth, Moldavite is a crystal that should be used with extreme caution. Though it will indeed set you on your intended path in life, it might not be the path you'd choose for yourself.

As one of the most powerful stones, Moldavite is able to eliminate any obstacles you come across on your journey, whether this be the wrong job, partner or home.

Selenite

CLARITY + CALMING + PURIFICATION

Need to find your inner peace?

Colleague made you cranky? Irritated over something that's out of your control? Find your inner peace with Selenite.

A purification and protection crystal, Selenite promotes mental clarity and wellbeing, with the ability to calm your mind with peaceful thoughts. This soul-lifting crystal is a must-have in stressful situations.

By placing crystals around your home you can actually transform its energy. The theory is that by having crystals in your home, you will raise the vibrations and fill your home with positive energy.

The thing about my crystal obsession
is that it doubles as high vibe home decor.

Green Aventurine

LUCK + PROSPERITY + OPPORTUNITY

Day out at the races?

Whether you're having a little bet or have an interview or test coming up, a little bit of luck goes a long way! Green like a 4 leaf clover and luckier than a rabbit's foot, Green Aventurine is known as the stone of opportunity.

Achieve your goals in life and inspire new ventures by keeping this stone around and making your intentions clear.

Pyrite
PROTECTION + STRENGTH + WILLPOWER

Need to avoid bad vibes?

When negativity and bad luck seems to be taking over your life, give it a good arse kicking with Pyrite! Despite being called 'fool's gold' due to its metallic appearance, this crystal really is no fool.

Not only does it have the power to protect its user from negative vibrations and energy, Pyrite also helps to boost your memory, willpower and strength of mind!

Blue John can only be found in Derbyshire, England. The mineral is a form of fluorite that contains bands of yellow and purple.

The stone is so brittle that it is infused with epoxy resin in a vacuum chamber before being polished into jewellery.

Natural Blue John

Sodalite

INTUITION + INSIGHT + CLARITY

Suspicious of someone in your life?

Has someone been screenshotting your messages in the group chat? When you need to weed out the backstabbers in your friendship group, Sodalite has your back!

Use Sodalite when you need to think rationally about a situation as it helps to boost your powers of observation and analysis.

Flourite

DIRECTION + CONFIDENCE + SELF-LOVE

Need a roadmap to success?

If you want to succeed and achieve the most in life, the Flourite crystal is a great tool to help you on your journey!

As a healing crystal, Flourite helps aid deep relaxation and improved energy levels, which is just what you need when you need to crack down on your concentration and focus. Whichever route you take in life, this crystal will help you slay!

The Cabochon Star Sapphire is also known as the star of Asia. The gemstone currently resides in Washington's Smithsonian National Museum of Natural History.

The 330-carat gemstone came from the Magok mine in Myanmar, the stone was given to the American museum in the 1960s by the Maharajah of Jodhpur.

Cabochon Star Sapphire

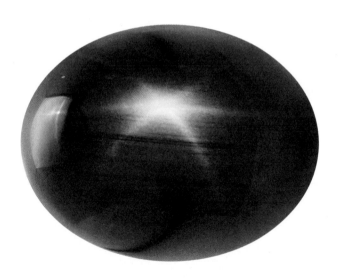

Emerald

LOYALTY + UNITY + PARTNERSHIP

Want to find a good balance in life?

If your boss is making you work overtime or your diary is full to the brim, you might have a lot on your plate. The Emerald crystal helps to achieve a physical, mental and emotional balance, so you can help to organise your busy schedule. Great at enhancing, this crystal provides inspiration, wisdom and patience to its user.

Known as the 'stone of successful love', Emeralds bring loyalty and domestic bliss to its user, as well as providing aid in your psychic abilities and promoting truth and deep knowing.

Chrysoprase

HEALING + LOVE + ACCEPTANCE

Want to patch up a broken heart?

Had your heart broken and need some help to get through it? Chrysoprase works wonders to heal a broken heart by enhancing love from friends and family, all while attracting new, worthwhile companions into your life.

This beautiful stone helps you to accept and let go, so you can say good riddance to your ex once and for all!

Most often, Quartz is found in granite, but sometimes people find it pure and clear. However, this happens infrequently as it requires the coincidence of a number of geological conditions.

Have a cheating ex and need someone who will appreciate you like you deserve? Get a Quartz.

Chalcopyrite

CONNECTION + MANIFESTATION + TRANSFORMATION

Want to become a real goal-getter?

Are you thinking about all the great things you want to achieve in life? Maybe it's a new project or hobby you want to take on. Whatever it is, you need to turn that dream into a reality! Turn your positive thoughts into actions with Chalcopyrite, a mystic transformation stone.

With the power to expand your mind, this stone enables its user to voice their emotions and manifest their thoughts, allowing them to make positive and life-changing decisions!

Moonstone

INTUITION + NEW BEGINNINGS + GROWTH

Need help balancing your emotions?

If you're feeling a little hormonal or have to work overtime for a big project, whatever you're feeling might be multiplied tenfold. Thought to harvest its energy from the moon's rays, Moonstone helps to soothe emotional instability, providing calmness and enhancing feminine energy.

With the ability to help improve inner growth and strength, Moonstone can help process your intuition. To keep your Moonstone at its most powerful, charge in the light of the full moon and receive its full potential!

books by
BOXER

www.booksbyboxer.com